HAVE A NICE DAY

A One Act Play

Lynn Brittney

Published by Playstage
United Kingdom

An imprint of Write Publications Ltd

www.playsforadults.com

Designed by Kate Lowe, Greensands Graphics
Printed by Creeds Ltd, Bridport, Dorset

Note to producers about staging "Have a Nice Day"

The set is simple. It is supposed to be the "green room" of a television station, where the presenters are made up and briefed on their programme. The set, therefore, should consist of office-type hospitality furniture, plus the make-up desk with a lit mirror. The television, which is facing away from the audience on a coffee table or low trolley, does not have to be working.

It is advisable for the technical crew to pre-record the "television interview", with its advertisement breaks and music, as one long piece and bring the volume up when the actors on stage are not speaking and take it down during the "advertisement breaks" when there is a lot of dialogue on stage.

The characters in the piece are suggested through hairstyles and clothing. KIRSTY – New Age hippy *(gypsy skirt, lots of ethnic jewellery, long hair perhaps)*; MARJORIE – harassed but businesslike *(trousers, jumper, nametag, clipboard etc.)*; JOE – perpetual undergraduate *(long hair, jeans, corduroy jacket etc.)*; CAROL – like so many "celebrities", wears dark glasses and dresses "down", expecting to be transformed by make-up and costume; DAVID – slick, smart, immaculate suit *(with perhaps a pink shirt and tie to hint at his flamboyant side)*.

HAVE A NICE DAY

CAST *(In order of appearance)*

KIRSTY   Slightly 'new-age- woman, amy age, make up artist.

MARJORIE   Harrassed producer, aged 40+

JOE   Clever, a bit of a 'nerd', researcher. Aged 40.

CAROL   TV presenter, dim, scrubs up well. Aged 20-30.

DAVID   Slick agent, smartly dressed. Aged 50+.

SIR WILLIAM
(offstage voice)   Elderly, well-spoken, intelligent

3 female and 3 male parts.

The action takes place in the 'green room' of a TV station.

HAVE A NICE DAY

The 'green room' of a television station. 8 a.m.

The programme to be presented is Have a Nice Day: a half-hour morning show presented by CAROL MORTON at 9 a.m.

The room contains a meeting table, with a pile of the day's newspapers and a phone on it. There is a sofa, and some chairs behind it. A low coffee table, is in front of the sofa, and there is a television set that faces away from the audience.

KIRSTY enters with a portable make-up mirror and a bag of make¬up and hairbrushes. She sets the mirror on the meeting table and starts laying out the brushes and the make-up.

MARJORIE enters, carrying a sheaf of papers and looking rather flustered.

MARJORIE   Has she still not arrived?

                (KIRSTY shakes her head and looks glum)

                Oh God. She must have read it by now.

KIRSTY   Well, she doesn't *normally* read the papers before she gets
                here.

MARJORIE   No. But it would be just our luck that the one day she
                decides to be well-informed would be today. Christ! It's all
                going to hit the fan when she does get here.

KIRSTY   *If* she gets here.

MARJORIE   No. She wouldn't do that. Whatever else I may think about
                her, I don't think that she would just not turn up.

(KIRSTY looks at her cynically)

Maybe I'd better warn Janice that she might have to carry on at nine.

KIRSTY   That'll make Janice happy.

MARJORIE   Oh God, I know, she's had no preparation at all. Thankfully, it's all devoted to the arty fella.

KIRSTY   You'd better get Joe to pull out the sheet on him.

MARJORIE   Yes. Have you got a fag?

KIRSTY   *(rummaging through her bag and producing out a pack of cigarettes)* Thought you were giving up.

MARJORIE   Not today, Kirsty. Not today. *(She spots the newspapers)* Oh Christ, I'd better get rid of those!
                      (MARJORIE scoops up the newspapers, but KIRSTY grabs the top one)

KIRSTY   Not until I've had one more read of the juicy bit.

MARJORIE   Kirsty!

KIRSTY   I don't think I've had such a good laugh in ages.

MARJORIE   That's cruel.

KIRSTY   Oh, come off it, Marjorie. It's absolutely wonderful, you know it is. And totally deserved. Is it true?

MARJORIE   What do you mean?

KIRSTY   The bit about her being axed.

MARJORIE   Dammit, I just don't know! That's what worries me.

                      If *I* don't know, then maybe I've got the bullet as well!

KIRSTY   Nah. It's not your fault Carol's useless. You didn't give her the job.

MARJORIE	Kirsty, you've been in television long enough to know that the people who are responsible for the cock-ups rarely take the blame.
KIRSTY	That's true. They usually pin it on some poor innocent sod and walk away.
MARJORIE	Exactly.
KIRSTY	Sorry.
MARJORIE	Oh God, it's so unfair! I've told them time after time that she's useless and they've just never paid any attention. Kirsty, read it out to me.
KIRSTY	*(reading from the paper)* "A little bird has told us that *Have a Nice Day* presenter Caroline Morton is about to get the elbow. Ratings have dropped as the nation has gone back to bed, bored by her silly smile, her feeble interviewing technique and her pastel-coloured jumpers. Rumour has it that Caroline Morton is to be replaced with someone a bit more gutsy, who knows enough about current affairs to be able to ask sensible questions. So, it's bye-bye to smiley Carol. Have a nice day, Miss Morton." God, it's right on the button, isn't it?
MARJORIE	D' you know, I'm sure that some of those descriptions are exactly what I wrote in my last memo. I bet some bugger's leaked it to the press.
KIRSTY	Wouldn' t be surprised. That's how most of the decisions get made around here.
	(JOE enters, putting his head around the door)
JOE	Carol's coming!
MARJORIE	Oh God!

KIRSTY	*(shoving the paper in her bag)* How is she?
JOE	Mad as hell.
MARJORIE	Oh God.
	(CAROL enters, pushing JOE out of the way. She is wearing black trousers, a black jumper and dark glasses. Her hair is tied back in a pony tail, and she has a fake fur coat on. She looks fairly scruffy.)
CAROL	*(To MARJORIE)* What have you got to say for yourself, you bitch?
MARJORIE	Carol—sweetie—I didn't know anything about this—honestly.
CAROL	In a pig's eye! You couldn't tell me to my face, could you, you vermin? You had to tell the bloody Sun first. Trying to save your own skin, I suppose.
MARJORIE	Now, how would giving a story like that to the Sun save my skin, Carol? Be reasonable.
KIRSTY	Yeah. Poor old Marjorie could just as easily get the chop for this.
	(CAROL looks at them both, then sits down and bursts into tears.)
CAROL	It's not fair! It's just not fair...
MARJORIE	*(putting her arm around CAROL)* I know, sweetie, I know.
CAROL	I mean, all I've done is do what I'm told in front of the cameras. I was *told* to wear pastel jumpers!
	(MARJORIE and KIRSTY look at each other. CAROL, as usual, has missed the point.)

KIRSTY	*(taking CAROL's hair out of its rubber band and starting to brush it)* I wouldn't take any notice of it, luv. I mean, the Sun's always having a go about someone. It doesn't mean anything. Joe, get Carol a cup of coffee.
JOE	Yeah. Right. *(JOE exits.)*
CAROL	*(sniffing)* That crack about me not being well-informed... I mean, you don't have to be David Frost to interview women who've had miracle babies, or to talk about the latest fashions, do you?
MARJORIE	*(unsure of how to answer)* N-no. But you do have to read up the research notes beforehand, sweetie. You have been known to make a few bloomers in the interviews, haven't you?
CAROL	*(angrily)* I knew you'd throw that in my face! I just got confused last week, that's all. I mean, not everyone knew that the President of the United States wasn't the President of the United States anymore—if you know what I mean.
KIRSTY	Yeah. It was only the main news item of the morning.,.
CAROL	Shut up and start my make-up!
	(KIRSTY moves to stand in front of CAROL. Throughout the following conversation, she concentrates on the make-up. JOE enters with the coffee, a file and a copy of the Sun)
MARJORIE	You see, slip-ups like that are remembered. And you have had one or two in your time——
JOE	Yeah. That one with the two mothers whose babies got swapped over in hospital was priceless. There they were, having been through this trauma and uncertainty, and Carol says to one of the mothers: "Actually, your baby does look

more like Mrs Smith than you. Are you absolutely sure you've got the right one?" I thought it was great.

CAROL   Who asked you, dog-face?

MARJORIE   Thank you, Joe. Have you got the notes for this morning's programme?

JOE   Oh, yes. Right. *(He starts reading from his notes.)*

            Sir William Forrest. Just been appointed director of the new Humbold Gallery. The gallery and the appointment have both been approved by Prince Charles, by the way.

CAROL   *(sulkily)* Oh, really, why?

JOE   *(looking at MARJORIE and raising his eyes to heaven)* Because Prince Charles likes the building. It looks nice and old — it's not horrible and modern, And he likes Sir William because he's a friend of lots of friends of the Royal Family.

CAROL   Oh, right.

JOE   Sir William is eighty four, and he went to Cambridge with lots of other luminaries — like Kim Philby. *(He laughs)*

CAROL   Why is that funny?

JOE   Jesus, I don't believe this!

CAROL   Don't patronize me, you pig! I said, "Why is that funny?"

JOE   Because Kim Philby was a traitor — a Russian spy.

CAROL   *(irritably)* I know that, so what?

JOE   Because all the other luminaries who were at Cambridge at the same time were a bunch of queers, public school weirdos and commies who all ended up in plum Establishment jobs because their daddies had lots of moncy and moved in the right circles.

KIRSTY   Joe's having one of his broad-minded days again...

JOE   I don't know why I do this sodding job. Preparing chimpanzees to take GCSEs would be easier.

CAROL   Piss off.

JOE   *(standing up and bowing sarcastically)*I shall do that small thing for you, Miss Morton. Thank you so much for your time. Dealing with an intellect like yours is what gets me through this grey existence of mine.

MARJORIE   *(wearily)* Cut it out, Joe. We've got enough problems today, without you getting precious on us. Sit down and carry on briefing Carol – I'll go to Wardrobe and pick out a few outfits. *(MARJORIE exits)*

JOE   *(sitting down again and speaking to CAROL like she is a small child)* Are you sitting comfortably? Then I'll begin.

CAROL   Cut the crap and get on with it.

JOE   *(taking a deep breath)* The Humbold Gallery is right in the centre of London, in the City——

CAROL   Where in the City?

JOE   Moorgate.

CAROL   Oh, that's where that wonderful shoe shop is. *(To KIRSTY)* Y' know, where I got those brown patent shoes with the little gold trim...?

KIRSTY   *(not really listening)* Mmm.

JOE   *(sarcastic again)* Perhaps the Humbold Gallery will open some franchises in its foyer. The odd Sock Shop or Tie Rack—something tasteful.

CAROL	*(defensive)* That's not so silly, you know. In my opinion, galleries and museums would attract a lot more people if they had some seriously cool clothes shops or eateries.
JOE	*(withering)* Quite a patron of the arts, aren't you? I bet you go to Glyndebourne every year with a Kentucky Fried Chicken Family Meal and a bottle of Mexican lager.
CAROL	*(annoyed)* You think you're so superior to everyone else, don't you?
JOE	No, not everyone else. Just you. Tell me, Carol, how did you get this job, anyway?
CAROL	You know very well how I got this job.
KIRSTY	*(reciting)* She was spotted presenting Playdays on CBBC...
CAROL	It was Blue Peter.
KIRSTY	Sorry.
JOE	Yes. I rest my case.
CAROL	Blue Peter is the longest-running children's show on television. Lots of intelligent TV presenters started their careers on that show.
JOE	*(not caring)* Really. I'll take your word for it. Can we get back to the Humbold Gallery?
CAROL	OK.
JOE	The Gallery is going to house all the Turners that have never been on public display – plus other Old Masters that are currently stored elsewhere. About bloody time too...
KIRSTY	Yeah.
CAROL	Why?
JOE	Pardon?

CAROL	Why?
JOE	Why what?
CAROL	*(exasperated)* Why is it about bloody time?!
JOE	Because Turner painted lots of wonderful paintings, which we, as a nation, paid a fortune for and they haven't been on show because no-one would cough up the money or find the space to hang them. Not to mention all the other Old Masters – that's paintings by famous artists who've been dead for a long time – for those who don't know – that we also paid a fortune for and no-one has ever seen.
CAROL	*(bluffing)* Right. I knew that.
JOE	Of course you did. I will continue with the briefing. The Humbold Gallery has been financed by Henry Begovich, which is ironic, and—before you ask why— I will tell you. Henry Begovich made a fortune on the money markets when the pound collapsed. And he used part of that fortune to build and endow the Humbold Gallery. So you could say that it was conscience money. The British economy suffered because of people like him, so the least he can do is give us a new art gallery. He'll probably get a knighthood out of it too.
KIRSTY	That's a bit simplistic, isn't it?
JOE	Kirsty, my dear, most things in life can be brought down to simple equations. Like, no-one gets rich without someone else paying for it, and there's no such thing as an altruistic entrepretneur.
CAROL	Does anyone know what colour this geezer's wearing? Only, I don't want to clash.

(JOE sighs and puts his head in his hands in despair)

KIRSTY   No, sorry. Don't know. I'll leave your lipstick until Marjorie comes back with the outfits.

CAROL   I'm not wearing anything that's pastel.

KIRSTY   I wouldn't take any notice of that newspaper article if I were you. You look lovely in pink.

CAROL   *(firmly)* I am *not* wearing pink. And I'm not doing it because of the article. I' m going to start doing what *I* want to do from now on. If I'm going to get the sack, it doesn't matter, does it?

JOE   *(giving up)* Oh, good! We'll forget Sir William Forrest then, and you can just make a spaceship out of old yoghurt pots or something, eh?

CAROL   *(irritated)* Oh, very funny. If you're so wonderful, how come you're not a presenter? I'll tell you why. Because people like to watch a programme that's presented by someone who's young, looks nice and who doesn' t make them feel stupid. And you are old, look like a pig and you spend your whole life trying to make people feel small.

JOE   My God—you just said a whole paragraph without an autocue. And for the record – forty is not old.

CAROL   Oh, shut up. I'm sick of you. I'll be glad to see the back of this programme, if I am going to get fired.

KIRSTY   Oh, give it a rest, you two! It's like being in a war zone every morning.

CAROL   *(sulkily)* Well, he started it. He always does. I'm fed up with people like him—and the bloody newspapers. I'm not going

	to let them get away with this. I'm going to sue them for every penny they've got.
JOE	You do realize that if you sue them for libel, you have got to prove that *they* are wrong?
CAROL	What are you talking about?
JOE	I mean, dear, that you have got to stand up in court and prove that you are not—*(he reaches for his newspaper and reads)* "a feeble interviewer who doesn't know enough about current affairs to be able to ask sensible questions"...
CAROL	*(uncertainly)* Well...
JOE	Exactly.

(DAVID SORREL enters. He is a smart-suited, slick man of 50+, who runs with the hares and the hounds. He throws his arms out to CAROL)

DAVID	Darling! I'm so sorry you've had a bad morning!
CAROL	*(bursting into tears and hugging him)* Oh, David! Thank God you've arrived. It's been so horrible. How could they say such awful things?
DAVID	There, there, pumpkin. Never take any notice of newspapers, darling.
CAROL	But I have to. They're saying I'm going to get the sack!
DAVID	Hmm. Well, we'll cross that bridge when we come to it, darling.
CAROL	When?
DAVID	Sorry—if.
CAROL	*(suspicious and slightly hysterical)* You know something, don't you? David—agents always know these things first—

don't they?

DAVID	Carol—sweetheart. *(To KIRSTY and JOE)* Can we talk privately, please, darlings?
KIRSTY	Of course.
JOE	You've only got fifteen minutes before you go on air.
DAVID	We'll only need five.
	(JOE and KIRSTY exit)
	Sit down, sweetheart.
CAROL	*(suspiciously)* What do you know, David?
DAVID	*(cagey)* Well, let's just say I've heard a little whisper— nothing more than that. A little whisper that the powers that be think you would be better suited to another show...
CAROL	*(eagerly)* They're going to give me a better job?
DAVID	*(hedging)* Well... They haven't actually made a firm commitment yet, but I have hopes.
CAROL	Why didn't you tell me all this? Why did I have to find out from the newspapers?
DAVID	Darling! I told you. It was just a whisper—nothing firm. I didn't really have anything to tell you. How the newspapers got hold of it, I don't know. These things happen.
CAROL	*(bitterly)* So it's true then. They don't think I'm any good.
DAVID	*(being reassuring)* Now, Carol, sweetie, that isn't the case at all! You're very popular, you know you are. Think of all your fan mail. The housewives love you.
CAROL	That's true. I'm always being sent jumpers and ear-rings. They always remember my birthday...
DAVID	*(wincing slightly at the memories)* And think of the time

you broke your leg presenting that skiing item. The hospital was swamped with flowers. And the time you crashed in the new Ford Sierra you were test driving...

CAROL   Yes. So why do they want to get rid of me?

DAVID   *(lowering his voice)* Well, between you and I, the station's in a bit of trouble. The competition's hotting up, and I've heard that they're considering making the morning slot into a hard news programme.

CAROL   *(eagerly)* But I could do that! I could do hard news!

DAVID   Sweetie, be reasonable. You've a pretty face with a charming personality, but, face it, you're not a news presenter.

CAROL   Why not? I've got great hair and skin – everyone says so. Good teeth, you know...

DAVID   Of course you do. What I mean is, you've had no news training—you're not a reporter.

CAROL   *(lamely)* I could learn.

DAVID   Best stick to what you know, sweetie. We'll find you a nice magazine prog to front.

CAROL   *(sniffling)* I was happy on Blue Peter...

DAVID   Ah, darling, you're too old for children's telly now—you know that, don't you?

        (CAROL nods and sniffles)

        I've heard that one of the northern stations is considering a lunch-time fashion slot. We might put you up for that——

CAROL   *(brightening)* North? What, Manchester?

DAVID   *(being evasive)* Er — a little further north than that, actually.

CAROL	How much further. . .?
DAVID	Er — the Hebrides, actually.
CAROL	The Hebrides!
DAVID	*(hastily)* Emerging local station, Carol — you could do worse.
CAROL	Not much worse, unless it's a bloody oil rig off the Norwegian coast! Are you serious?
DAVID	Well, no. On second thoughts they probably wouldn't want a presenter with an English accent. These Scottish stations are very parochial.
CAROL	*(disgusted)* Is that the best you can come up with — a lunch-time slot in the bloody Hebrides?
DAVID	Look, sweetie, you've caught me on the hop here. I haven't had a chance to do some lunches and find out what's going down in telly land.
CAROL	Well, you'd better do some lunches damn quick and get me out of this mess. I've got a London flat and a villa in Italy to pay for, you know. What is the matter with everyone? I'm treated like dirt by people here, and now my own agent is treating me like last night's leftovers!
DAVID	Carol, you're upset. You're not thinking clearly...
CAROL	Am I not? I feel as though I'm thinking very clearly indeed. In fact, the penny's just dropped... *(accusingly)* You've known about this for some time now, haven't you? In fact, I wouldn't mind betting that you've been weaselling some other client of yours into my job, haven't you? Haven't you?
DAVID	Darling, can I help it if so many of my clients are TV presenters? One of them is bound to be in the running for any job that you may vacate ——

CAROL   I bet. I just bet. You slimy toad. All you care about is your
             bloody percentage. If you don't get it from me, then you'll
             make damn sure you get it from someone else.

DAVID   Sweetie, be reasonable. We're all in business to make
             money...

CAROL   *(furious)* Don't you sweetie me, you poisoned piece of——

             *(MARJORIE enters. She is laden down with pastel-coloured
             jumpers and skirts)*

MARJORIE   *(from behind all the clothes)* Carol, make a selection from
             this lot quickly, love, time is getting short.

CAROL   *(grabbing the clothes and hurling them across the room in a
             fury)* I'm not wearing any of them ! In fact, I'm never
             wearing another pastel bloody jumper as long as I live.
             You're all a bunch of creeps and I'm not listening to any of
             you ever again.

             *(CAROL picks up the newspapers from the desk and
             proceeds to tear them up. JOE and KIRSTY enter, standing
             in the door to witness the scene)*

             (Emphasising her words as she tears the papers) I'm —
             never — going to trust — anyone in this bloody — industry
             — again. I'm going to — do — what — I — want — to do
             — and sod — everyone — else. I'm sick — sick — sick —
             of — everyone — and everything...

             *(She stands there panting from her effort. The room is in
             total chaos, covered in bits of torn newspaper and clothes.
             Pause)*

             (To KIRSTY) Give me your ear-rings.

             (No-one moves)

I said give me your ear rings!

(KIRSTY removes her large dangly ear-rings and hands them to CAROL)

Now your pendant. Come on, come on, the pendant!

(KIRSTY removes the pendant and hands it over. CAROL puts the jewellery on, then scrapes her hair back in the rubber band and puts on some very dark lipstick)

Right. Shall we go?

MARJORIE	Carol, you can't go on set dressed like that!
CAROL	Just shut it. I'm *going* on set like this, and that's an end to it. OK?
MARJORIE	Oh God.
CAROL	Where's that bloody crib sheet?

(JOE silently hands over a sheet of paper)

(To JOE) Just watch me now, dog-face. Just watch me.

(CAROL exits)

KIRSTY   Just look at this place! She really went to town, didn't she? *(She starts to clear up)*

JOE   *(dryly)* I've never seen her so animated. Perhaps there are hidden depths.

MARJORIE   Oh, shut up, Joe. What the hell is she going to do? David, what did you say to her?

DAVID   Absolutely nothing, sweetie. I just came here to do my sympathetic Uncle David bit.

JOE   I bet. You probably just came to wave your percentage bye-bye.

DAVID	You're far too cynical, mate. That's why you'll always be a researcher.
JOE	Bollocks.
MARJORIE	Oh, shut up. It's two minutes to nine. *(She sits down and turns on the TV set)*
	(JOE sits next to MARJORIE, and DAVID stands behind them. KIRSTY continues to clear up. CAROL's voice is heard)
CAROL'S VOICE	After the break, I will be interviewing Sir William Forrest, director of the new Humbold gallery. Join me then.
	(During the following exchange we hear various adverts on the TV set)
MARJORIE	God, she looks a total mess. Upstairs are going to kill me; letting her go on set looking like that.
JOE	Actually, she looks right for the part.
MARJORIE	What do you mean?
JOE	Well, you know, she looks sort of—arty. You know, sort of scruffy stylish—black clothes and ethnic jewellery. Just right to interview the director of an art gallery.
MARJORIE	*(worried)* Do you think so?
DAVID	*(thoughtfully)* Actually, dear boy, I think you've got something there... Where's the phone?
JOE	What are you up to?
DAVID	Just had one of my brilliant ideas, sweetie. *(He reaches for the phone and makes a call)* Hallo, darling. Be a sweetie and get me Lazard Productions, will you? Have you got the

number? Good, I'll hold. *(He pauses)* Hallo, Angela? David Sorrel here. Be a sweetie and put me through to your revered boss, will you? You're an angel, *(He pauses)* Hallo, Tarquin, you old reprobate. Long time no lunch, eh? *(He laughs)* Well, usually you move in too rarefied a circle for me, old darling. But listen, I might just have something for you. That late night arts programme you're putting together... Yes... I think I've got a presenter for you... No, really. Just switch your set on to Have a Nice Day and then call me back in ten minutes. Just *do it*, will you, lovey, for old David, and give me a ring back. I'm in Suite 7 at the AMTV studio. OK?

(The Have a Nice Day music plays)

CAROL'S VOICE	Good-morning. Today I am devoting the whole programme to an interview with Sir William Forrest, newly appointed director of the latest and most spectacular art gallery in London—the Humbold Gallery.
JOE	Well, at least she got the name right.
MARJORIE	Shut up.
CAROL'S VOICE	Good-morning, Sir William.
SIR WILLIAM'S VOICE	Good-morning.
CAROL'S VOICE	I'd like to ask you about the aims of the gallery and your own involvement in its development in just a moment. But

first, I'd like to ask you a rather personal question. This gallery is the first new gallery we have had in London for nearly fifty years. Do you not think that it would have been better if it had been fronted by a younger man than yourself?

MARJORIE   Oh, my God!

JOE   Holy shit!

KIRSTY   Whoops.

DAVID   Bugger.

(There is a brief silence and everyone stares at the television)

SIR
WILLIAM'S
VOICE   *(chuckling slightly; good-humouredly)* Well, I think that's a frank and fair question which deserves an equally frank answer. In one way, yes, I do think a younger man should have been appointed. I' m a bit of an old war horse and should have been put out to pasture years ago. But, in another way, there is method in their madness. Old war horses like me are unflappable, even in the thick of battle, and the Humbold Gallery is going to be fighting for a few years for recognition and money, and I guess the powers that be thought I was the chap to see the gallery through the tough times until it was established. We are just about to appoint some young wizard to be my second-in-command, of course. That's the way to train young horses, you know, harness them to the old placid ones like me.

JOE   Brilliant.

MARJORIE   Thank God.

CAROL'S
VOICE   Would it be fair, Sir William, to say that you got the job because of your Establishment connections? I mean, you went to the right school and then to Cambridge, and so on...

JOE   I think she's gone too far now.

MARJORIE   Oh God...

SIR
WILLIAM'S
VOICE   *(good-humouredly)* But of course! Going to the right school and university are of inestimable value in my work. I know all the right people, all the sources of money— *(he laughs)* even the right people to blackmail, if it came to it.

JOE   This guy is a gem.

            (The phone rings and DAVID picks it up)

CAROL'S
VOICE   It seems that the Humbold Gallery is indeed fortunate to have your services. Tell me, does the source of initial finance of the gallery bother you at all? The fact, I mean, that it was financed by someone who profited from a disastrous collapse in the British economy?

DAVID   Yes, I'm holding...

SIR
WILLIAM'S
VOICE   God, no! It won't be the first time, or the last that our nation's heritage is financed out of so-called conscience money, or, as is the case with many of our art endowments, as a tax dodge. Mr Begovitch has made no secret of the

source of his wealth, which I think is very courageous of him.

It's probably cost him a knighthood to admit he profited in that way. But we have gained something of true worth in the process.

DAVID   Tarquin—wasn't I right? Isn't she brilliant?

JOE   You're joking! Bloody lucky, more like.

CAROL'S
VOICE   We are now going to look at a short film about the gallery as it prepares for its grand opening to the public next month. After which we will return to a further conversation with the director, Sir William Forrest.

MARJORIE   *(getting up and turning down the volume of the TV set}* I think it's going remarkably well, I really do. Don't you?

DAVID   *(into the phone)* Well, she's looking for a change, Tarquin. Frankly, she's under-used here, and it's not her forte...

JOE   *(incredulous)* Do you believe this guy? He could sell the Pope as a presenter of Swedish porn programmes.

DAVID   She'd want more money, of course... Look, let's do lunch today. I've just discovered a divine bistro in Wardour Street. Right up your alley, old darling. Wall to wall opera. Mozart and meatloaf, that sort of thing,.. Good. I'll see you in your office at one. Ciao. *(He hangs up)*

JOE   *(to DAVID)* And just how, pray, are you going to get away with Carol as a major arts programme presenter? What she knows about art you could write on the head of a pin.

DAVID   *(putting his arm around JOE's shoulders)* Well, sweetie it just so happens that my old mate Tarquin is looking for a Head of Research for this new programme.

JOE | What? Me, work with Carol again? You must be joking! We can't stand the sight of each other.

DAVID | Ah, but luvvy, you make such a good team, and we are talking serious money here. Tell me, John——

JOE | Joe.

DAVID | Joe—have you got an agent?

(DAVID takes JOE into a huddle in the corner)

MARJORIE | Kirsty, have you got another fag?

KIRSTY | *(rummaging through her bag and producing cigarettes and a lighter)* Why don' t you just start up again? It would save me a fortune.

MARJORIE | Sorry. Oh God. Why did I ever become a producer?

KIRSTY | Because you're mad.

MARJORIE | *(with a heartfelt sigh)* Yes.

(DAVID and JOE come out of the huddle and shake hands enthusiastically)

DAVID | Well that's settled then! Welcome aboard Team Carol, Joe. If anyone can guide her through the arts world, it's you.

JOE | I just hope I can keep my sanity, that's all.

DAVID | Ah, well. If this deal goes through, you'll be able to afford the very best psychiatrists – so don't worry. *(Looking at KIRSTY and MARJORIE)* Well girls…I think we should repair to the champagne bar across the road and down some bubbly, don't you?

KIRSTY | *(gathering up her things)* Count me in! I'm always up for a free spot of bubbly.

MARJORIE   *(brightening up)* I'm game!

JOE   Shouldn't we watch the rest of the programme?

              (Everyone else looks at each other amd pulls a face or shakes their head.)

EVERYONE   Nah...Not really...not bothered...etc.

JOE   *(shrugging)* OK.

              (They all proceed to exit – then MARJORIE pauses and speaks to DAVID)

MARJORIE   What shall we drink to?

DAVID   *(smiling broadly)* Oh I don't know...how about 'Television – the medium of truth'?

MARJORIE   *(snorting)* Don't be silly, David!

BLACKOUT.

Have A Nice Day music plays.

FURNITURE AND PROPERTY LIST

Property fittings required: nil Interior. The same throughout

On stage:	Meeting table. On it: newspapers, phone
	Sofa Chairs
	Low coffee table
	Television set
Offstage:	Portable make-up mirror (KIRSTY)
	Bag. In it: make-up, hairbrushes, cigarettes, lighter (KIRSTY)
	Sheaf of papers (MARJORIE)
	Cup of coffee (JOE)
	File (JOE)
	Newspaper (JOE)
	Pastel-coloured jumpers and skirts (MARJORIE)
Personal:	Earrings, pendant (KIRSTY)

LIGHTING PLOT

To open: Overall general lighting No cues

EFFECTS PLOT

Page 17   MARJORIE : CUE : "Oh shut up. It's two minutes to nine."
               She turns on the TV set.
               CAROL's voice as per script.

               CAROL's VOICE : CUE : "Join me then."
               TV adverts start playing until….

Page 18   DAVID : CUE: "I'm in Suite 7 at the AMTV studio. OK?"
               Adverts stop. Have A Nice Day music plays.
               Followed by CAROL's voice as per script. Television
               interview
               Continues until p.21 (see below).

Page 20   JOE: CUE: "This guy is a gem."
               Telephone rings.

Page 21   CAROL's VOICE: CUE: …"further conversation with the
               director, Sir William Forrester."

               MARJORIE turns down TV volume.

Page 23:   MARJORIE: CUE: "Don't be silly, David!"

               Have A Nice Day music plays.